Where Is the Colosseum?

by Jim O'Connor

illustrated by John O'Brien

Grosset & Dunlap
An Imprint of Penguin Random House

In memory of the Flavian Emperors—
Vespasian, Titus, and Domitian—who
built the Colosseum—JOC

For Terase—JOB

GROSSET & DUNLAP
Penguin Young Readers Group
An Imprint of Penguin Random House LLC

Library of Congress Cataloging-in-Publication Data is available.

ISBN 9780399541902 (paperback)   10 9 8 7 6 5 4 3 2 1
ISBN 9780451533609 (library binding)   10 9 8 7 6 5 4 3 2 1

Contents

Where Is the Colosseum?

It is AD 80 and the streets of Rome are buzzing with excitement. The new emperor has promised one hundred days of games to celebrate the opening of an amphitheater that stands in the center of the city.

It is named the Flavian Amphitheater after the emperor's family and is a marvel of engineering. It is huge, over 150 feet high, and will seat fifty thousand people. There are eighty entrances that quickly funnel spectators to their correct seats. There are snack bars, many water fountains, and even indoor bathrooms.

A massive canopy stretches over the open-air arena and provides shade for the crowd. It is operated by a team of one thousand sailors who can haul the canvas cloth canopy—a huge fabric roof—into position and adjust it as needed.

Today's show begins with battles between men and wild animals. The animals—lions, tigers,

bears, and elephants—have been brought from every corner of the Roman Empire. In the next hundred days, more than nine thousand animals will be slaughtered.

Later, at lunchtime, prisoners will be brought from jail to be torn apart by some of the animals or killed by soldiers. Although it is hard for us to understand, the crowds find this entertaining. The people of ancient Rome devoured this sort of spectacle—the bloodier the better.

The high point of the day comes in the afternoon—pairs of fighters called gladiators will fight each other with deadly weapons. People in the crowd root for whichever gladiator they want to win. They scream and cheer. Again, it is hard for us today to think of people killing each other as entertainment. But to the Romans, it was.

The grand opening of this huge arena marks a climax in the history of ancient Rome. The amphitheater is the largest ever built. Soon it will come to be called the Colosseum. Today, two thousand years later, it is a ruin. Yet it is still one of the most famous sites in all of Rome, in all of Italy. More than five million people visit every year to see a reminder of the bloody power of one of the world's greatest empires.

CHAPTER 1
How Rome Began

By the time the Colosseum opened, the city of Rome was almost eight hundred years old.

According to legend, Rome was founded in 753 BC by Romulus. Romulus and his twin brother, Remus, were the children of a human woman and Mars, the Roman god of war. Their mother, Rhea, left her twins to die in the Tiber River. But the twins floated down the river and were saved by a she-wolf. The wolf took care of the babies in a nearby area with seven hills.

According to one legend, when they grew up, the twins wanted to build a city on one of the seven hills. But they could not agree on which hill. Neither twin would give in and there was a terrible fight. Romulus killed Remus.

Romulus built his city exactly where he wanted and named it Rome, after himself. The people who lived there came to be called Romans.

Roman Gods

The ancient Romans believed in many gods. Each god or goddess had different powers and duties. These were the twelve main gods:

• Jupiter was the king of the gods and, according to legend, the twin brother of Juno.

• Juno was the goddess of marriage.

• Venus was the goddess of love and the mother of the Roman people.

• Vesta was the goddess of hearth and home.

• Ceres was the goddess of agriculture and human fertility.

MERCURY

- Diana was the goddess of the hunt.
- Minerva was the goddess of wisdom.
- Mars was the god of war.
- Vulcan was the god of fire.
- Mercury was Jupiter's youngest son and also the messenger of the gods.
- Apollo was the god of the sun.
- Neptune was the god of the sea.

NEPTUNE

Over the next three hundred years, Rome grew so large that it covered all seven hills. It grew up along the banks of the shallow Tiber River.

Around 400 BC, Rome founded Ostia, a harbor city on the coast. From there Roman ships could sail to all the trading centers on the Mediterranean Sea. The Romans grew rich.

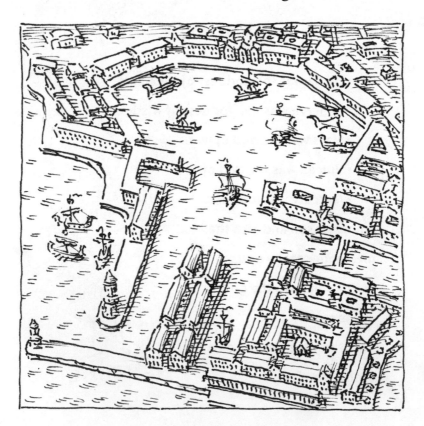

By 218 BC, Rome had conquered all of what is now the country of Italy. By AD 117, the Roman Empire stretched from Britain in the north through most of Europe and included all the land around the Mediterranean Sea. Countries that are today known as Turkey, Iraq, Iran, and Saudi Arabia were all part of the Roman Empire. The Romans brought their way of life to these conquered lands.

After every conquest, the victorious Roman general would return home and parade through the city, showing off the riches he'd taken as well as the many prisoners of war. The riches from conquered lands paid for massive building projects like the Colosseum.

CHAPTER 2
Emperors

Who ruled over this vast and mighty land?

One man—the emperor.

It wasn't always that way. For nearly five hundred years, Rome had been a republic. The word *republic* comes from the Latin term "res publica," which means "property of the people."

In a republic, power is held by the people—not one ruler. The people elect representatives to govern them. In Rome, there was a senate—a group of men who made the laws.

But then in 49 BC, that changed. One man, Julius Caesar, was most responsible for ending the republic.

JULIUS CAESAR

Caesar was a great general, a talented politician, and a gifted author. His books about his military campaigns are still read today.

Caesar was very popular with the citizens of Rome. The Senate, however, saw him as a threat. They were right to be scared. In 49 BC, Caesar and his followers started a civil war. After winning victories against his fellow Romans, Caesar got the Senate to name him dictator for life in 46 BC. From then on, whatever he wanted became law. But only two years later, he was killed by enemies right inside the Senate building.

After Caesar came Augustus, who was the first man to be called emperor. An emperor ruled by controlling the Senate. The senators could give advice to the emperor, but he did not have to listen to them.

AUGUSTUS CAESAR

Even more important, an emperor's power came from having a massive army behind him. So the emperor worked hard to keep the army happy and loyal to him. Augustus was very popular with both the Senate and the army. He ruled the Roman Empire for forty-five years.

The next four emperors ruled for a total of fifty-four years. Mostly, it was a time of peace. So the era became known as the "Pax Romana" or Roman Peace. But emperors were always fearful of being overthrown by enemies. They did not even trust family members, and sometimes had them killed.

Nero was the last of the five emperors that came after Caesar. He ruled from AD 54 to 68.

Nero was cruel and very corrupt. He had his mother executed because she was plotting against him. He also had his stepbrother poisoned.

NERO

Today Nero is known for playing the fiddle while watching Rome burn.

The fire in AD 64 was terrible. It lasted nine days and destroyed much of the city. The story about Nero and his fiddle, however, is not true. In fact, Nero helped search for survivors and wanted the city to be rebuilt as quickly as possible. He even paid for some of the work with his own money.

At the same time, Nero took a huge piece of land in central Rome for himself. There he built the most magnificent palace ever seen. The palace had over three hundred rooms, including a banquet room that revolved. There was an artificial lake,

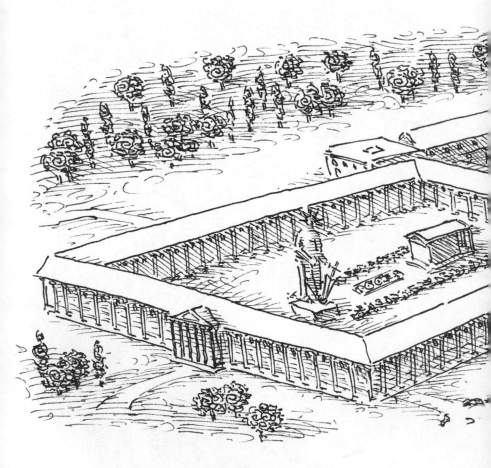

vineyards, and orchards. The outside of the palace was covered with rare seashells and precious gems, and painted in some places with gold leaf that reflected the sun. For that reason it was named the "Golden House."

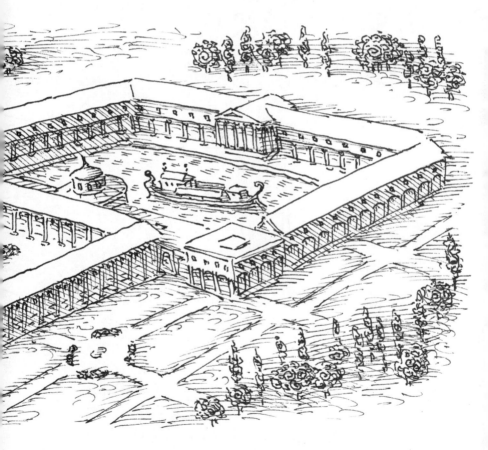

A statue of Nero, 120 feet tall, stood at the entrance to the house. A statue that big is called a colossus. Today we still use the word "colossal" to describe something huge.

When Nero moved into his Golden House, he said, "Now I can at last begin to live like a human being." But he didn't get to enjoy his fantastic palace for long. In AD 68, he was overthrown and killed himself.

The year after Nero's death, four men fought one another to become the new emperor. The winner was a popular general named Vespasian. It was Vespasian who got the idea to build the Colosseum—the biggest amphitheater in the world. It would be a symbol of Rome's strength and power, one of the wonders of the ancient world.

VESPASIAN

The Seven Wonders of the Ancient World

Seven amazing structures were famous throughout the ancient world. Early guide books spread their fame far and wide. Each of them was unique in its size and purpose.

• The Great Pyramid of  Giza (around 2560 BC) is the oldest of the Seven Wonders and the only one that still exists. It is just outside Cairo.

• The Hanging Gardens of Babylon (around 600 BC) were in what is now called Iraq. Legend says that King Nebuchadnezzar II built the Hanging Gardens for his wife because she missed the green hills and mountains of her home.

• The Temple of Artemis (around 550 BC) was built at Ephesus to honor the Greek goddess of hunting. The temple was rebuilt three times before it was permanently destroyed in AD 262.

• A giant statue in Olympia, Greece (around 450 BC), portrayed Zeus, the king of the Greek gods, seated on an elaborate throne.

• The marble Mausoleum at Halicarnassus was a magnificent tomb for King Mausolus. The modern word for "tomb," *mausoleum*, comes from the king's name.

• The Colossus of Rhodes was a gigantic bronze statue, believed to be ninety-eight feet high, that depicted the Greek god Helios. It stood at the entrance of a harbor and was destroyed by an earthquake in 226 BC.

• The Lighthouse of Alexandria (280–247 BC) was in Egypt. It was around 380 feet tall and was the model for other lighthouses. Three earthquakes, in AD 956, 1303, and 1323, destroyed it.

CHAPTER 3
Roman Arenas

Why did the Romans like brutal and bloody entertainment? One reason may be that they believed they were descendants of Mars, the god of war. They took pride in being warriors. In those days, soldiers fought face-to-face with short swords and spears. Winning battles and conquering new lands made the empire ever greater.

MARS

When Roman soldiers came home from war, they missed the excitement of the battlefield. So sometimes for entertainment, Roman soldiers would form a square and force two prisoners to fight each other until one was killed.

In time, these "contests" grew. They would be sponsored by rich men, perhaps as a way to honor their dead relatives. At first only two or three pairs of gladiators would fight. Later the contests became larger and more expensive. Temporary wooden arenas would be built, then taken apart afterward.

More gladiators fought. Soon free food was given to the spectators. Fighting and killing became

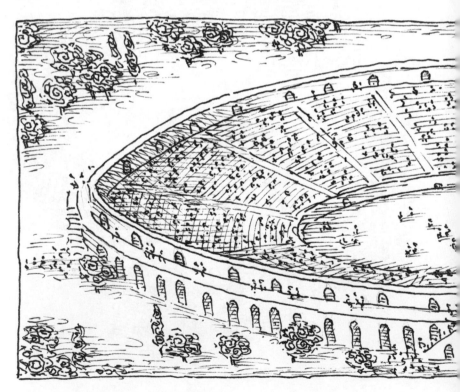

part of Roman culture.

The first permanent, stone amphitheater was built in Pompeii around 80 BC. It held twenty thousand people. Like the Colosseum, it was oval in shape, but it was dug into the ground. From the street it appeared quite small. Once spectators walked into the stadium, they saw how much bigger it really was.

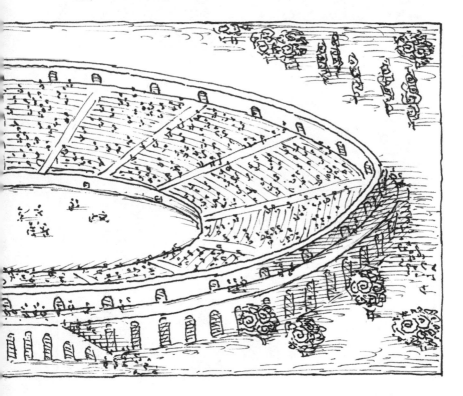

When Mount Vesuvius erupted in AD 79, the amphitheater was buried in volcanic ash. Pompeii was rediscovered in the late sixteenth century, and work to excavate the city began in 1748. Pompeii has the oldest and best preserved of Roman amphitheaters.

CHAPTER 4
The Work Begins

Where did Vespasian decide to build the new arena?

Right in the middle of Rome.

He chose a spot in a valley between two of Rome's hills. It was where Nero had created the lake. That was why Vespasian chose the spot. He wanted to erase any trace of the hated Nero. (He is said to have had the face on the colossal statue of Nero changed and a crown added so it looked like a god.)

Before any construction was able to begin, Vespasian had to get rid of the lake. This was done by draining the water through underground tunnels into the Tiber River.

After that, the foundation of the amphitheater

DRAINING THE LAKE

could be built. It had to be strong enough to support the enormous stone structure Vespasian planned. After more than thirty thousand tons of earth were dug out, concrete was poured in, mixed with layers of gravel.

Concrete

Concrete had been invented by the Romans hundreds of years earlier. It was made of gypsum, lime, volcanic ash, water, and aggregate. The aggregate contained small stones, broken ceramic tile, and brick rubble from demolished buildings. Roman concrete, because of its volcanic ash content, is actually more durable than modern concrete.

It took about two years before the foundation was completed. In AD 72, the amphitheater began to rise.

Most of the construction was done by slaves. Historians estimate that about a hundred thousand slaves worked on the project, on the site or in the stone quarries. Most probably came from Judea, which Vespasian had conquered before he became emperor.

No one knows who the architect was. The design seems simple. Basically, the Colosseum is an oval made with a tall outer wall. Inside are sloping tiers of seats that lead down to the arena in the center at ground level. (The word "arena" comes from the Latin word *harena*, meaning a sandy place. The Romans used sand to give gladiators good footing but also to absorb blood.)

The Romans built many amphitheaters throughout their empire, and the ruins of some of them are found in North Africa, Spain, France, and Italy. The colosseum in Nîmes, France, built around AD 100, is still in use today for bullfights and rock concerts. It only holds 16,300 people, but resembles the Roman Colosseum with its many arched windows and entrances.

COLOSSEUM AT NÎMES

Modern Stadiums

Today many stadiums around the world are much larger than the Colosseum.

The Los Angeles Memorial Coliseum was built in 1923 and is where the University of Southern California plays football games. Used for both the 1932 and 1984 Olympics, it can hold almost 80,000 people.

China's Beijing National Stadium which has seating for 91,000 spectators was built for the 2008 Summer Olympics. Its interwoven metal beams make it look like a giant bird's nest—which is what many people call it.

The largest stadium currently in use is the Rungrado May Day Stadium in Pyongyang, North Korea. It can seat 150,000 spectators.

BEIJING NATIONAL STADIUM

What made Vespasian's amphitheater so special was its size. Although there are only four levels, it is as tall as a modern-day fifteen-story building. The ground-level arena is 180 feet across and 287 feet long. That is wider and also almost as long as a football field.

Vespasian wanted his amphitheater to open during his lifetime. To speed up work, he divided the building into quarters, with a different construction team for each section. This did

TITUS

speed up the work. Yet even so, when Vespasian died in the year 79, construction had only reached the second level. It was up to the next emperor, Vespasian's older son Titus, to continue the job.

Titus opened the Colosseum in AD 80. He had gladiators fight wild animals, and gladiators fight other gladiators. But supposedly he also staged sea battles in the Colosseum. He had the arena flooded and brought special flat-bottomed ships in because the water was so shallow. The ships were smaller than regular Roman galleys but they were propelled by oarsmen and carried trained fighters who were expected to kill their opponents in the other ships.

Domitian, the next emperor, was not interested in staging sea battles. Instead he had the area under the arena rebuilt to hold scenery for the games, cages for the wild animals, and cells for the prisoners who were to be publicly executed. There were trap doors in the arena's floor. A system of pulleys raised the scenery in place. Other trap doors let the tigers, bears, and elephants into the arena where they would fight against gladiators.

Domitian's changes made the "circuses," as the spectacles were called, more exciting. Animals could suddenly appear through the ground. New gladiators charged out to fight matches. The audiences demanded bigger and bloodier circuses and, in order to keep them happy, the emperors gave them just that.

CHAPTER 5
A Close Look at the Colosseum

The Colosseum was built primarily from three different materials: limestone, brick, and concrete.

Travertine, the main type of limestone used, is heavier and stronger than bricks or concrete. It was cut from a quarry about twenty miles from Rome. Travertine was used for columns and wherever carved stonework was needed.

Large slabs of travertine were also used for stairs and most of the seats. But they were not made on-site. Stairs and seats were built in workshops

around Rome. They were all the same size so they could be used wherever needed. The stairs and seats would be delivered to the building site and installed.

Raising the heavy travertine into place was one of the most difficult jobs. The Romans used a crane powered by men who walked inside a huge wooden wheel. As they walked, the wheel turned and wound a rope around an axle. This shortened the rope and raised the stone to the correct location where the builders could slide it into place.

Concrete formed the guts of the Colosseum. It was mixed right at a building site. Concrete is easier to work with than marble. It is also lighter than stone.

For all the vaulted arches of the passageways and corridors, the Romans first built wooden molds. Then they poured the concrete into the molds and let it harden.

Vaulted arches made the ceilings much stronger than flat ceilings. The concrete arches added strength to the building but not much weight. Without concrete, the Colosseum could not have been made as large as it was.

Bricks were only used for decorative purposes on the arches and some of the corridors.

Roman Arches

The ancient Romans were the first engineers to use arches and barrel vaults extensively in construction. An *arch* is a curved structure used for doorways and hallways. An arched doorway is much stronger than a simple flat-topped doorway.

An arch is held in place by the weight of all its stones. Building an arch is difficult. The most

KEYSTONE

WOODEN SUPPORT

common way is to build a wooden frame that follows the curve of the underside of the arch. The individual stones are laid on it until all are in place. The stones stay supported until the center stone, called the keystone, is inserted. Then the wooden frame is taken away.

Barrel vaults are simply a series of archways placed next to each other to form hallways.

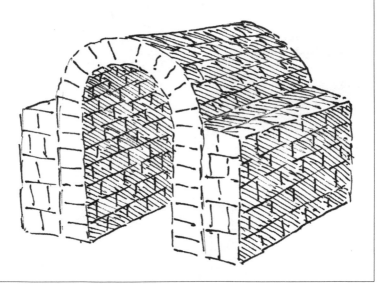

Columns (round pillars used for support) appear throughout the Colosseum. However, ones on the outside were only for decoration. They did not actually help hold up the building.

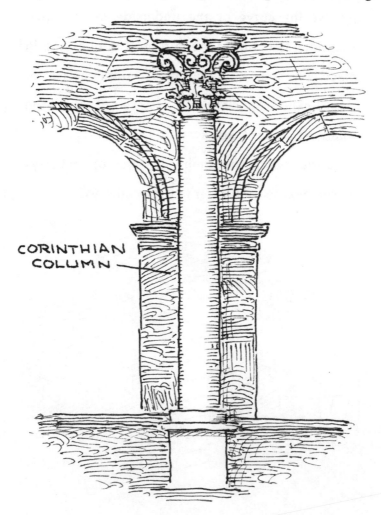

CORINTHIAN COLUMN

Also decorating the outside were 160 painted statues of emperors and gods. No two were the same. Each was fifteen feet tall and stood inside an arch on the second and third levels of the Colosseum.

The original plan for the Colosseum called for only three levels. Titus, Vespasian's older son, decided to add the fourth level after Vespasian died. The fourth level is not as fancy as the other levels. However, it allowed many more Romans to sit and watch the circuses in the arena.

CHAPTER 6
The Audience

Inside the Colosseum were five separate seating zones for spectators. Where people sat was determined by how important they were. The best seats in the stadium, the ones nearest the arena, went to the rich and powerful.

Big shots sat in a marble terrace called the podium. At one end of the arena was the royal box. The emperor, the male members of his family, the head priest, and special guests sat there. Opposite it, at the other end of the arena, was a box for the empress and her attendants.

Next came the seating areas for senators, ambassadors, famous military leaders, and priests of various important temples.

The third zone was the largest section, with

THE ROYAL BOX

nineteen rows and seats for 20,400 spectators—ordinary Roman citizens.

Above that area were seven rows for freed slaves, foreigners, the poor, and regular slaves. It sat about 10,000 spectators.

The highest six rows of seats were reserved for women—the wives and daughters of senators

THE SEATS FOR
WOMEN

and other important citizens. This space offered women protection in bad weather and, because there was a high stone wall in front of the seats, some privacy from the poor ticket holders just below them. Women may also have been placed so high to shield them from the blood, gore, and screams of the arena.

All spectators had tickets made of animal bone, wood, or lead with the number of their seating section and their seat numbers. Very often free tickets were given to poor Romans to keep them loyal to the emperor. Sometimes the sponsor of a circus paid for all the seats to gain favor, and votes, if he was running for office.

Ordinary spectators entered through one of seventy-six numbered gates. Each entrance led to stairs or ramps that brought the spectators to their seats. As they moved through the Colosseum, the spectators passed snack bars, drinking fountains, and bathrooms.

The hallways and galleries were all decorated with stucco murals. Circular galleries allowed people to move all the way around the amphitheater.

Very few visitors to the Colosseum today realize that once there was a giant awning called a *velarium* at the very top of the amphitheater. It protected spectators from the strong rays of the Roman sun.

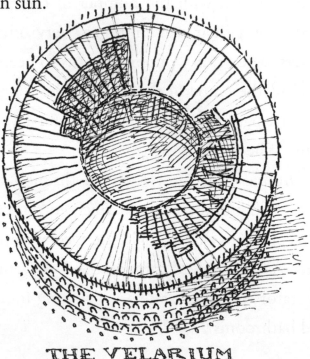

THE VELARIUM

Raising the velarium was an epic undertaking. One thousand sailors were needed to do the job. One hundred and sixty pulleys were attached to wooden poles along the walls at the very top of the building. The center ring of the velarium supported the web of ropes for the awning. It was laid in the middle of the arena. Then ropes were run up through the pulleys and down the outside of the Colosseum to 160 winches attached to stone blocks.

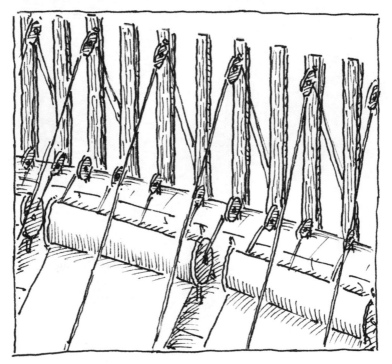

Each winch was turned by a team of four or eight sailors. All the ropes raising the ring had to be pulled in unison. A drummer would beat time so all the winches would turn together and raise the ring evenly.

When the ring was raised to the top of the Colosseum, the ends of the ropes were tied down on the winches. Then a second set of ropes was run from the pulleys beneath the first set of ropes and tied to the center ring. The canvas strips that formed the velarium were then unrolled onto the lower web of ropes and tied together. The finished awning weighed many tons.

The center of the ring remained uncovered so that sunlight filled the arena.

The Colosseum was also designed to let spectators get out quickly in case there was an emergency. Some archaeologists have estimated that all fifty thousand guests could leave in under ten minutes!

Wild animals also posed a threat to the emperor and people sitting closest to the arena. Although it is believed that the wall around the arena was twelve feet high, some animals, like lions and tigers, could jump higher than that.

So sturdy nets were strung from poles stuck into the arena floor several feet from the wall. This made it much harder for a leaping animal to reach the wall. In addition, the walls of the arena were made of highly polished, and very slippery, marble. And even if an animal could leap over the net and onto the top of the wall,

there were ivory rollers that spun when touched. They prevented an animal from getting a good grip, thus stopping it from jumping into the crowd.

As a final safety measure, skilled archers were stationed all around the arena, ready to shoot any animal before it became a threat.

CHAPTER 7
The City of Rome

In ancient times, the Colosseum was only one of the major public buildings in the great city of Rome.

Near the Colosseum was the Forum, or Forum Romanum. It was the center of Roman life. The Forum was built around an open area where teachers held classes and merchants sold goods

THE FORUM

from stalls. Politicians and other Romans met there to talk and gossip. There were temples to the goddess Vesta and the god Vulcan. There were also temples for emperors, including Caesar and Vespasian and Titus. On one side of the Forum was the Basilica, the court of law where people accused of crimes came for trial. The Curia, which was the senators' meeting hall, was nearby.

THE BASILICA

Today tourists can walk through the Forum Romanum and see the ruins of many temples and other buildings as well as some triumphal arches— monuments built after great victories in battles.

City Plan

The city of Rome was not laid out in a grid like later Roman cities. That's because it grew up helter-skelter over many centuries. Its streets twist and turn. It is often difficult to find your way from one place to another.

Later Roman cities like Pompeii all followed the same plan. They were laid out like a chessboard with a gate on each side and two main intersecting streets. Each block was exactly eighty yards long on every side. The typical block would have several private houses, some retail shops, an apartment building, and a workshop.

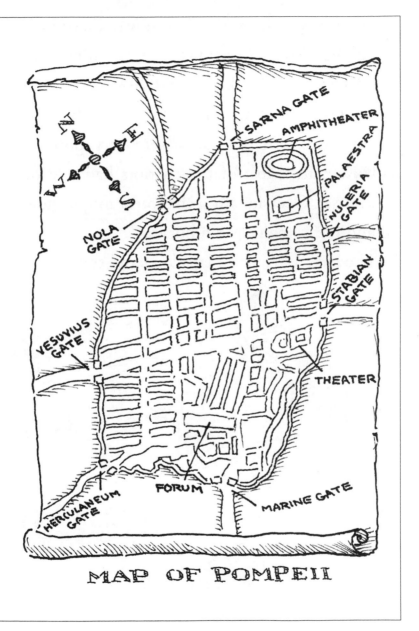

MAP OF POMPEII

Not far away from the Forum was a racetrack called the Circus Maximus. It was more than 2,000 feet long and held 250,000 people. Like the Colosseum, it was a sports arena—but for chariot races. Chariot races were very popular with Romans. Most of the chariots had two or four horses. Occasionally a charioteer might show off and use as many as ten horses.

The races were seven laps long and there were

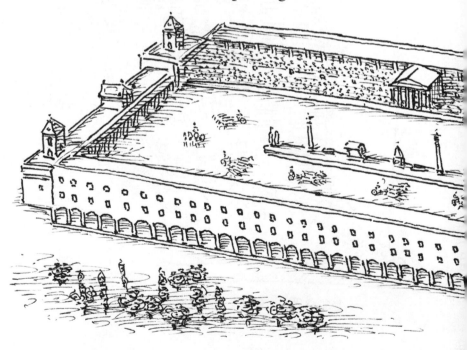

as many as twenty-four races a day. A single race covered more than three miles.

Roman charioteers tied their horses' reins around their waists. This was extremely dangerous. If a chariot crashed, the driver would usually be dragged to his death—unless he could cut the reins.

Besides horse races, the Circus Maximus was used for religious festivals. There were staged hunts for wild animals, gladiator fights, and public executions.

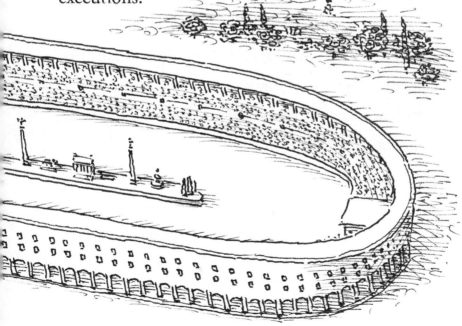

Romans enjoyed seeing plays and by the time of the Colosseum, Rome had two main theaters. The Theater of Pompey was the first stone theater. Although there is almost nothing left of Pompey's theater, the ruins of the Theater of Marcellus can still be seen. It could seat between eleven thousand and twenty thousand spectators and resembles the Colosseum with its many arched entrances and arches on the second floor.

Romans liked to see both comedies and tragedies. The writer Lucius Annaeus Seneca, called Seneca the Younger, became famous for his tragedies. Nine of them have survived to modern times. Some are still performed, including *Medea*, *Phaedra*, and *Oedipus*.

Roman society did not think very highly of actors. All were men and had a bad reputation— so bad, in fact, that Emperor Tiberius made it illegal for actors to be friends with the upper classes.

THE THEATER OF
MARCELLUS

Most Roman homes, even those of the rich, did not have baths. So big public baths were built and used by rich and poor alike. The baths usually had one area for men and a separate area for women.

Inside each were changing rooms, exercise areas, and three rooms of different temperatures: a hot steamy room, a warm room, and a small circular room where men could plunge into a cold pool. (The women's section of a bathhouse did not have a pool. Instead, they could take a cold bath in their changing room.)

The bathhouses also are proof of what incredible engineers the Romans were. Furnace rooms heated the water and piped it to the different baths. Hot air from the furnaces was channeled under the stone floors of the warm and hot rooms. The floors got so hot that bathers had to wear wooden-soled flip-flops to protect their feet.

The public baths were not only about getting clean. They were another place where Romans went to socialize. They could meet up with friends, gossip, argue about politics, or discuss horse races they'd seen at the Circus Maximus.

All these public spaces in Rome had something in common. They were ways to keep the people of Rome content. Happy people were unlikely to rebel against the emperor.

Cemeteries

One thing you would not find in any ancient Roman city was a cemetery. All cemeteries had to be outside the city walls. Although most Romans were cremated at that time, not even their ashes were allowed to remain in the city. They were considered a health hazard.

Rich Roman families built elaborate tombs on both sides of the roads leading into the city. The more desirable spots cost more than ones farther away from the city.

Some tombs were designed with benches so that visitors had a place to rest.

People who had no families could join burial societies that arranged for a member's funeral and burial. Gladiators also had burial societies to make sure their bodies would be treated with respect and that friends could honor them. Sometimes the gladiator's gravestone gave a record of his wins and losses.

CHAPTER 8
Lifestyles of the Rich and Not So Famous

At the height of the empire, about a million people lived in Rome. Like all the other cities of the empire, rich and poor lived side by side, often on the same block. Of course, it was much more pleasant to be rich than poor.

Wealthy Romans lived a life of ease and pleasure. They owned large, airy homes with their own kitchens, running water, and sometimes even baths.

In the front part of the house was an open-air room called the atrium. Wealthy Romans often used their homes to conduct business. Customers and clients would wait in the atrium until the owner could see them.

In the center of the atrium was a shallow pool that collected rainwater from the roof. The water was used for cooking and washing.

Most often, bedrooms were located off the atrium. They were usually small and dark because they did not have windows. Crime was always a

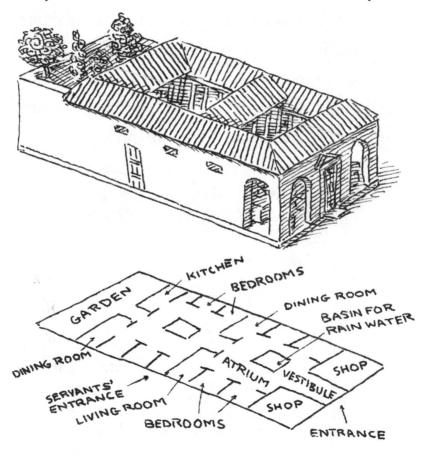

concern in Rome, so if there were windows facing the street, they were small, high up, and had thick iron bars to keep intruders out.

Larger houses also had a dining room called a triclinium.

Floors in grand homes were often covered with mosaics. A mosaic is a picture made of colored bits of glass or stone, known as tesserae (say: TESS-uh-ree). In some houses, a mosaic in the entrance hall would show a picture of a snarling dog with the words *Cave Canem* ("Beware of Dog").

Frescos in bright colors—blues, greens, and reds—might decorate the walls. A fresco is a picture that is painted directly onto wet plaster. The plaster dries, cementing the painting onto the wall.

The walls around the house's garden might have a fresco painted to look like wild nature. The family could pretend they were out in the country and not in a crowded city!

Of course, most Romans were not wealthy and could not afford large, lovely houses. Sometimes entire families were jammed into very small spaces. Some homes of the rich had two small rooms facing the street. These were rented out to shopkeepers. Goods were sold in the front room, and the shopkeeper's family lived in the cramped back room. All shops were locked at night with heavy wooden shutters to keep out robbers.

Most Romans lived in apartment buildings. They had only one or two rooms and no ovens or running water. People could go to local food

AN APARTMENT BUILDING

shops and buy precooked food. They could get stews, beans, fish, and cheese. Romans could eat in the shops or bring the food home. So even in ancient Rome, there were take-out restaurants!

Most neighborhoods had a bakery where Romans could take their bread dough and have it baked. Roman bread was round and indented into eight sections so it could be easily cut. Roman bakeries were very busy and had huge ovens. When the ruins of Pompeii were discovered, eighty-one loaves of bread were found in one oven!

There were also taverns where Romans could buy wine to go with their meal. And there were many fountains where very poor Romans could fill jugs of water for mealtime.

Like all human beings, Romans needed to drink water to live. In addition, they needed fresh water for cooking, watering plants and gardens, and bathing. At first Rome relied on wells. However, the water from various springs that fed the wells was not safe for drinking. River water from the Tiber became polluted. So the first aqueduct to serve Rome was commissioned in 312 BC.

An aqueduct looks like a bridge held up by columns that go across a valley. Aqueducts carry clean water to faraway places. As the population grew, the Romans built more aqueducts to bring in water from distant lakes. By the late third century AD, Rome had eleven different aqueducts.

The aqueducts were carefully planned. They had to have a slight downward slope from beginning to end to keep the water moving. The water channel was covered to keep out dirt and trash that could pollute the water.

Most were built about fifty feet above the ground. This prevented people from stealing water or, worse, poisoning it. When the water reached the city, it was collected in reservoirs (huge basins). Gravity provided the water pressure

to move the water through pipes to fountains, the baths, and even some private houses.

The very last building to go up in a Roman city was the amphitheater. Every sizable city had one, although none as grand as the Colosseum.

Roman Streets

The streets in Rome, unfortunately, weren't ever washed down. They were filthy. All the household garbage, including human waste, was dumped into the streets every day. All that garbage and waste sat in the streets rotting and smelling worse and worse. At the same time, horses and oxen pulling wagons also produced a lot of manure. It mixed with the household garbage for days or weeks until finally a rainstorm came and washed everything into the gutter drains.

Because of the filth, stepping stones were built in the streets. They stood higher than the roadway. Romans could cross without ruining their sandals and getting their feet filthy. Some Roman women wore special shoes or boots for walking through the city. They were followed by a slave carrying their nice sandals. Once they reached their destination, the women would change into their good shoes.

CHAPTER 9
Gladiators

Most people who visit the Colosseum know something about the bloody fights between gladiators, men who often fought to the death in front of fifty thousand screaming fans.

It is important to remember that almost none of the gladiators were volunteers. They were prisoners of war, slaves, or condemned criminals.

A very few men, however, did choose to become gladiators. Why would anyone decide to do this? Usually they were men who wanted regular meals and a roof over their head. And there was a slim chance of surviving and winning some money.

Early gladiator shows only had fights between two or three pairs of gladiators. Yet by the time of Julius Caesar, "games" could feature a hundred or more pairs fighting over two or three days.

Providing training for gladiators became a profitable business. Promoters founded gladiator "schools" where men were trained to fight and kill. Before training began, the men were examined by a doctor. The school wanted to be sure that a new man was healthy enough to bother training.

Usually a gladiator learned only one way to fight. Some were trained with a net and three-pronged spear called a trident. Such a fighter was called a *retiarius*. Except for a shoulder guard, they wore no armor. Very often a *retiarius* would be matched against a kind of gladiator called a *secutor*. The *secutor* carried a short two-edged sword and a rectangular shield. He wore a helmet that was rounded so that the *retiarius's* net could not snag on it.

Thracians, named for the Mediterranean land of Thrace, fought with

TRIDENT

A RETIARIUS FIGHTING A SECUTOR

short curved swords and carried small circular or square shields. They wore a wide-brimmed helmet with a visor.

Hoplomachi carried a short thrusting sword, a dagger, and a six-foot lance. Thracians often fought against *hoplomachi* who wore heavy armor. This offered some protection from the weapons of the Thracians. But armor slowed *hoplomachi* down, so they were pretty evenly matched with the quick-moving Thracians.

A HOPLOMACHUS FIGHTING
A THRACIAN

Samnites, named for a region of ancient Italy, carried a short sword and a long rectangular shield. They wore plumed helmets with visors. They also wore metal armor on their lower left legs, and a cloth or leather *manica* (guard) on their right arm. A Samnite was sometimes matched against a *retiarius* or other Samnites.

SAMNITE

Bestiarii only fought wild animals. They were armed with a spear and a knife and sometimes a whip. They had a visored helmet, and their arms and legs were wrapped in cloth or leather. Sometimes they might have a very small shield.

The *bestiarii* received special training to fight wild animals like lions, tigers, and bears. Their schools were called Schools of the Morning (*Ludus Matutinus*) because the wild animal fights were always held early in the day.

Gladiators always entered the arena from the Gate of Life. There was another gate on the opposite side of the arena. It was called the Gate of Death.

In the afternoon, gladiators marched into the arena wearing purple cloaks. Purple was the emperor's color. Musicians marched behind them blowing war trumpets. When circling the arena, the gladiators stopped in front of the emperor's box. Together they shouted, "We who are about to die salute you." Then they went to put on their armor and wait to be called back into the arena to fight and, perhaps, die.

Several pairs of gladiators would fight at the same time in different parts of the arena. Gladiators were usually matched according to the number of times they had fought. So new fighters would face others with little experience. This was fair, and also guaranteed a close, action-filled fight.

When one fighter was exhausted or badly wounded, he'd throw down his shield and raise a

finger of his left hand. This was a signal asking for mercy. The emperor decided if the man lived or died. But he also let people in the crowd give their opinion. The audience voted with their thumbs. If they made one gesture, the gladiator lived. If they gave another, the emperor signaled to the victorious fighter to cut his opponent's throat.

Most gladiators did not survive for very long. But successful gladiators

were the rock stars of the Roman empire. Children played with clay gladiator "action figures." There were posters with their pictures around the city. And women loved them. One piece of graffiti in Pompeii said a certain gladiator was "the delight of all the girls." If a skillful and lucky fighter won enough bouts, he was allowed to retire. He was given a wooden sword, called a *rudis*, as a symbol of his freedom.

CHAPTER 10
The Colosseum through the Ages

After it opened, the Colosseum hosted events for another two hundred years. Although few matched Titus's hundred days of games, in AD 107, Emperor Trajan sponsored 123 days of games in the Colosseum to celebrate his victory in the Dacian War. Five thousand pairs of gladiators fought, and eleven thousand animals were killed.

TRAJAN

Usually emperors sponsored games. Ones paid for by politicians were never as lavish as those sponsored by emperors. It was not smart for anyone to try to show up the emperor.

Sponsoring games was expensive. Importing animals and keeping them fed cost a lot. Getting gladiators was also expensive. The gladiators were "rented" from a gladiator school. Contracts were made and signed.

The men who owned the gladiators wanted to protect their investments. So often, the sponsor agreed that most of the losers would be shown mercy.

In AD 325, Emperor Constantine, a convert to Christianity, banned gladiator combat. But Constantine did not enforce this ban at all strictly, and gladiator contests continued in the empire until 404. Executions of criminals and wild animal fights were held in the Colosseum until 523. By then Rome's glory days were over.

EMPEROR
CONSTANTINE

Constantine moved the capital of the Roman Empire to Constantinople early in the fourth century. Rome was no longer the center of the empire. Now Constantinople got all the money that would have gone to Rome's budget. By this time, the Colosseum was already over 250 years old and, like any old building, it needed repairs and maintenance. It got almost nothing.

Earthquakes in the ninth and thirteenth centuries collapsed the outer walls on the south side of the building.

As the Colosseum deteriorated, so did Rome. Once a bustling city of more than a million people, by the end of the sixth century, the population was as low as thirty thousand.

Before long, Romans began to use the Colosseum as a handy source of building materials. When earthquakes knocked marble slabs off the Colosseum, Romans took many of the slabs to use on their own homes.

People began to move into the Colosseum to live rent-free. Houses and barns were built. Gardens were planted. Blacksmiths set up forges. Soon parts of the amphitheater disappeared from view completely. Later on, part of the building was rented as a glue factory. It was also used to store manure.

By the twelfth century, the original purpose of the Colosseum had been forgotten. One guidebook identified it as a temple to the sun god.

At the end of the fifteenth century, the Catholic Church began putting on yearly religious plays in the Colosseum. In 1519, a chapel was built inside and a large wooden cross was erected. A pulpit was erected in 1744 from which monks gave sermons every Friday.

One of the popes took over two thousand cartloads of stones from the amphitheater for use in the church buildings. Some of the marble ended up in St. Peter's Basilica in Rome.

ST. PETER'S BASILICA

The elaborate painted walls were destroyed, and trees grew in the arena. The wooden floor fell apart. Visitors could peer down into the underground area and not realize that at one time, wild animals and prisoners had been kept there before they were killed.

In the 1870s, the government of Italy took back the Colosseum and made the Catholic Church leave. The chapel and Stations of the Cross and other religious additions were pulled down. Sixteen centuries worth of dirt and rubble was cleared out of the building. Trees and plants were uprooted and removed.

Some needed structural repairs were done. But there was no sign of the Colosseum's former glory. The building had lost everything, including the 160 statues that had stood in the arches on the second and third levels. Part of the outer wall was gone. There were no seats left anywhere. All that remained was most of the concrete structure.

Fortunately, during the 1800s, travelers began visiting Rome again. The amphitheater became a popular stop on tours. Writers and artists were inspired by the ruins. The view of Rome from the top of the Colosseum was magnificent.

The great English writer Charles Dickens visited in 1846 and wrote, "To climb into its upper halls, and look down on ruin, ruin, ruin all about it . . . is to see the ghost of old Rome."

World War II

In the 1930s, the Italian dictator Benito Mussolini installed some seating in the Colosseum so he could hold political rallies there. During World War II, the Colosseum served as a weapons warehouse and as a bomb shelter for Romans.

BENITO MUSSOLINI

Since the mid 1900s, archaeologists have been uncovering many more of the Colosseum's secrets. In 2008, a piece of marble was discovered near the amphitheater. Archaeologists believe it came from a statue of an emperor on a horse that once was above the Colosseum's royal entrance.

In 2011, a mosaic was found showing the god Apollo, and in 2013, graffiti was discovered. Both of these were covered with a thick layer of dirt and rock.

Every year, more than five million people visit the Colosseum. They marvel at its size and imagine the great stadium as it once was—gleaming in the sun while wild animals roared and men faced each other in deadly combat.

It is the battered symbol of the glory of the Roman Empire.

Timeline of the Colosseum

753 BC	Rome said to have been founded by Romulus
264 BC	First Roman gladiator matches on record
c. 80 BC	Amphitheater at Pompeii built
AD 69	Vespasian becomes emperor and begins planning the Colosseum
79	Vespasian dies and his older son, Titus, becomes emperor
	Mount Vesuvius erupts and buries Pompeii
80	The Colosseum opens with one hundred days of games sponsored by Titus
81	Titus dies suddenly and Domitian, the next emperor, completes the Colosseum
325	Emperor Constantine, a convert to Christianity, bans gladiator matches
1231	An earthquake hits Rome and knocks down the south outer wall of the Colosseum
c. 1500	Pope leases out part of the Colosseum for businesses and allows people to remove marble from the building
1825	Work begins to reinforce the Colosseum's walls
1870	The Italian government begins a cleanup of the Colosseum
1992–2000	Major renovation of the Colosseum takes place
2013	Roman graffiti discovered in a Colosseum passageway